D0503673

# What Do You Know About Dolphins?

## Harley Chan

Dolphins swim in the sea.
What do you know about dolphins?

# Do you know how a dolphin breathes?

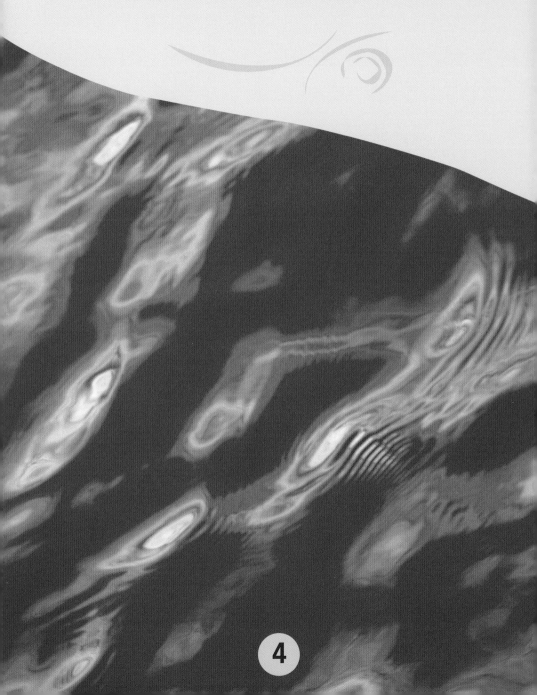

A dolphin breathes
through a hole in its head.
A dolphin comes
above the water to breathe.
It holds its breath
under the water.

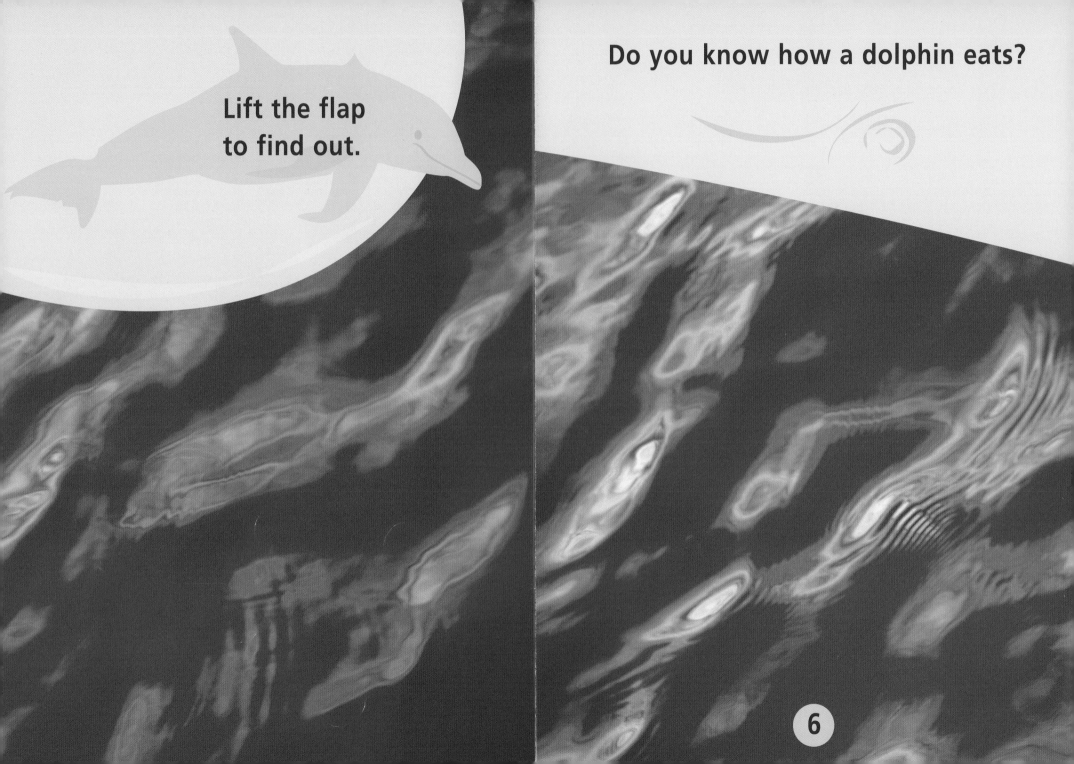

Lift the flap to find out.

Do you know how a dolphin eats?

6

A dolphin has lots of small teeth.
It uses its teeth to hold its food.
A dolphin eats its food whole.

Lift the flap
to find out.

Do you know how a dolphin swims fast?

8

A dolphin moves its tail fin
up and down to swim fast.
Its smooth body helps it swim fast.

9

Lift the flap
to find out.

Do you know what else
a dolphin can do with its tail fin?

10

It can stand on its tail fin.

# Index